# SURVIVE AND THRIVE: HOW TO GET READY FOR THE NEXT FINANCIAL CRISIS

RAY CYNERS

This book is designed to be a useful and informative resource. It provides general information and should not be construed as individual financial advice. The author is not responsible for any loss, damage or risk incurred as a result of reading this work.

Copyright © 2024 Ray Cyners
All rights reserved.
ISBN: 9798332371639

# CONTENTS

**Chapter One: Understanding Financial Crises** ..........1
   Historical Examples and Their Impacts ..........3

**Chapter Two: Assessing Your Current Financial Health** ..........13
   Evaluating Your Income, Expenses, and Debts ..........13
   Understanding Your Net Worth ..........14
   Creating a Personal Financial Statement ..........14
   The Importance of Regular Financial Assessments ..........15

**Chapter Three: Diversifying Your Income Streams** ..........16
   The Benefits of Multiple Income Sources ..........16

**Chapter Four: Smart Investing During Uncertain Times** ..........21
   Investment Strategies for Volatile Markets ..........21

**Chapter Five: Managing Debt Effectively** ..........29
   Prioritizing and Paying Off High-Interest Debts ..........29

**Chapter Six: Protecting Your Assets** ..........33
   The Importance of Insurance ..........33

**Chapter Seven: Cutting Costs and Budgeting Wisely** ..........37
   Identifying and Eliminating Unnecessary Expenses ..........37
   Creating a Flexible Budget ..........38
   Tips for Frugal Living ..........39

**Chapter Eight: Staying Informed and Adapting** ..........41
   The Importance of Financial Literacy ..........41
   Resources for Staying Updated on Economic Trends ..........41
   Adapting Your Financial Plan as Needed ..........43
   Monitor Key Economic Indicators ..........43

**Chapter Nine: Planning for the Long Term** ..........47
   Setting Financial Goals ..........47
   Retirement Planning in Uncertain Times ..........49
   Estate Planning and Protecting Your Legacy ..........49

**Chapter Ten: Psychological Preparedness** ..........52
   Coping with Financial Stress and Anxiety ..........52
   Building Resilience and a Positive Mindset ..........53
   Seeking Professional Financial Advice When Needed ..........53

**Chapter Eleven: Rebuilding Your Financial Foundation** ..........55
   Repairing Credit ..........55
   Setting New Financial Goals ..........56

**Conclusion: Navigating Financial Crises with Resilience** ..........57
**About the Author** ..........59

# Introduction

In an increasingly volatile global economy, being prepared for future financial crises is important for maintaining financial stability and peace of mind. The world has witnessed numerous financial upheavals, from the Great Depression to the 2008 Global Financial Crisis, each leaving a profound impact on individuals, businesses, and entire economies. These events underscore the importance of proactive financial planning and readiness for potential economic downturns.

One of the most compelling reasons for being prepared is the unpredictability of financial crises. They often strike without warning, and the ramifications can be swift and severe. Job losses, plummeting stock markets, and tightening credit conditions can all occur rapidly, leaving those unprepared in a precarious situation. Having a robust financial plan in place can mitigate the shock and provide a cushion to weather the storm.

The geodynamics in the political sphere among countries, as well as initiatives to create or adopt new common currencies, and thereby distance themselves from the dollar, create a scenario where potential financial repercussions are high, impacting both populations and governments.

The importance of being prepared for future financial crises cannot be overstated. The economic landscape is fraught with uncertainties, and the ability to navigate through financial turbulence is a testament to the foresight and planning of individuals and businesses. By diversifying investments, building emergency funds, managing debt, staying informed and regularly reviewing financial health, one can significantly mitigate the impacts of economic downturns. Proactive preparation ensures that when the next financial crisis hits, it is met with confidence and resilience, safeguarding one's financial future and providing peace of mind amidst the inevitable uncertainties of the global economy.

# Chapter One: Understanding Financial Crises

A financial crisis is a situation where the value of financial institutions or assets drops rapidly, leading to widespread economic disruption. This often results from a combination of factors, including excessive debt, risky financial practices, economic shocks, poor financial policies, speculative bubbles and a sudden loss of confidence among investors. Their ripple effects can cause severe impacts on economies, such as sharp declines in stock markets, bank failures, and a reduction in consumer wealth, leading to decreased spending and investment.

Financial crises often lead to significant downturns in the economy, causing recessions, high unemployment rates, and widespread financial hardship. They can affect anyone, from individual households to large corporations and governments, making it essential to understand what they are and how they occur.

Governments and central banks typically respond to financial crises with a range of interventions aimed at stabilizing the economy. These measures can include injecting liquidity into the banking system, lowering interest rates, and implementing fiscal stimulus packages. Despite these efforts, the aftermath of a financial crisis can lead to long-term changes in economic policies and regulatory frameworks to prevent future occurrences.

The immediate effects of a financial crisis on the population can be profound and far-reaching, impacting various aspects of daily life and overall economic stability. One of the most direct impacts is a surge in unemployment rates. As businesses face declining revenues and tighter credit conditions, many are forced to lay off workers or freeze hiring. This leads to widespread job losses and increased job insecurity for those still employed.

With rising unemployment and job insecurity, household incomes often decline. People may experience pay cuts, reduced working hours, or loss of bonuses and benefits. The reduction in income makes it difficult for families to meet their financial obligations, leading to a depletion of savings and, in severe cases, increased indebtedness.

As people lose jobs or fear potential job losses, they tend to cut back on spending. This decline in consumer spending exacerbates economic contraction as businesses experience lower sales, leading to further layoffs and potential business closures. The cycle of reduced spending and business decline can deepen the crisis.

Financial crises often hit the most vulnerable populations the hardest, leading to an increase in poverty levels. Those without savings or access to social safety nets are particularly affected. Inequality may also rise as wealthier individuals with more assets or diversified income sources are better positioned to weather the crisis compared to lower-income families.

Another effect is the instability in the housing market. Homeowners may struggle to meet mortgage payments, leading to an increase in foreclosures and evictions. Housing prices may fall, reducing household wealth and leading to negative equity, where the value of a home drops below the outstanding mortgage balance.

Banks and financial institutions, facing their own liquidity challenges, may tighten lending standards. This restricts access to credit for both consumers and businesses. People may find it harder to obtain loans for homes, education, or other personal needs, while businesses may struggle to secure funding for operations and growth.

The stress and uncertainty caused by financial crises can have significant effects on mental and physical health. Increased financial strain can lead to higher levels of anxiety, depression, and other stress-related conditions. Health care access may also become more challenging if people lose employer-sponsored health insurance due to job losses.

Economic hardship and rising inequality can lead to social unrest. People may become more frustrated with the government and financial institutions, leading to protests and other forms of social discontent. In extreme cases, prolonged economic distress can lead to political instability.

Financial crises can also affect educational opportunities, as families may struggle to afford tuition and other educational expenses. Students may drop out of school to support their families, impacting their long-term career prospects and perpetuating cycles of poverty and economic hardship.

Governments often respond to financial crises with austerity measures or fiscal stimulus packages. Austerity measures can lead to cuts in public services, affecting health care, education, and social welfare programs. Conversely, stimulus packages may aim to mitigate the crisis's impacts but can also lead to increased public debt.

The immediate effects of a financial crisis on the population are multifaceted, affecting employment, income, consumer behavior, housing stability, mental and physical health, access to credit, and overall social stability. The severity and duration of these impacts depend on the crisis's depth and the effectiveness of governmental and institutional responses.

## Historical Examples and Their Impacts

### The Great Depression (1929-1939)

The Great Depression is one of the most severe financial crises in history. It began with the stock market crash of 1929 and led to a decade-long economic downturn. Unemployment rates soared, banks failed, and millions of people lost their savings. The global economy was deeply affected, and it took years for many countries to recover.

It spanned from 1929 to 1939 and was one of the most severe economic downturns in modern history, primarily centered around the United States but with global repercussions.

The causes of the crisis can be defined as:

- **Stock market crash**. The crisis began with the Wall Street Crash of October 1929, where stock prices collapsed dramatically, leading to a loss of investor confidence and widespread panic selling.

- **Bank failures.** The crash led to numerous bank failures as panicked depositors rushed to withdraw their savings, causing a liquidity crisis and further exacerbating economic instability.

- **Global economic factors.** International trade and finance were disrupted by protectionist policies, tariffs, and a decline in global economic activity, contributing to the spread of the crisis beyond U.S. borders.

Among the impacts, we can highlight the following:

- **Unemployment and poverty.** The Great Depression resulted in soaring unemployment rates, with millions of people losing their jobs. Poverty levels rose sharply as families struggled to make ends meet.

- **Business failures**. Many businesses collapsed due to reduced consumer spending, decreased demand for goods and services, and credit shortages, further deepening economic hardship.

- **Banking crisis**. A wave of bank failures wiped out savings for countless individuals and businesses, leading to a loss of confidence in the banking system.

- **Social impact.** The depression had profound social consequences, including homelessness, hunger, and social unrest. It strained families and communities, leading to increased rates of mental health issues and social instability.

Governments implemented various policies to mitigate the crisis, including public works programs, unemployment relief, and financial sector reforms. The New Deal initiatives in the United States under President Franklin D. Roosevelt aimed to provide relief, recovery, and reform to revive the economy.

The long-term effects were:

- **Regulatory reforms.** The Great Depression prompted significant regulatory reforms, including the establishment of deposit insurance (FDIC), securities regulation (SEC), and social welfare programs to prevent future economic catastrophes.

- **Shift in economic thinking.** The crisis led to a re-evaluation of economic theories and policies, with greater emphasis placed on macroeconomic management, fiscal stimulus during downturns and the role of government in ensuring economic stability.

- **Global impact.** The Great Depression had lasting effects on the global economy, influencing international trade patterns, economic policies and geopolitical relations for decades to come.

The Great Depression was a monumental financial crisis that reshaped economic thinking, policy frameworks, and social structures worldwide. Its enduring legacy serves as a stark reminder of the devastating consequences of unchecked financial speculation, inadequate regulation and the importance of proactive government intervention during times of economic distress.

## Black Monday (1987)

Black Monday refers to October 19, 1987, when global financial markets experienced a severe crash, primarily affecting stock markets in the United States. This event is considered one of the most significant one-day market crashes in history. The stock market crashed triggering global financial instability and investor panic.

The causes associated to this crisis are outlined below:

- **Overvaluation and speculation.** Stock prices had risen sharply in the preceding years, fueled by speculative trading and high valuations, particularly in the technology and financial sectors.

- **Program trading.** Automated trading programs, known as program trading or portfolio insurance, exacerbated market volatility by triggering large sell-offs when preset conditions were met, amplifying the downward spiral.

- **Global economic factors.** Concerns over global economic stability, including trade imbalances and geopolitical tensions, contributed to investor unease.

**As consequence, the stock Market Plummet.** The Dow Jones Industrial Average (DJIA) dropped by 22.6% in a single day. Stock markets around the world, including those in Europe and Asia, also experienced significant declines, reflecting the interconnectedness of global financial markets.

The rapid and steep decline in stock prices led to widespread panic among investors, triggering a loss of confidence in financial markets. Moreover, financial institutions and brokerage firms faced severe liquidity problems and potential insolvency due to the market crash. Central banks, including the Federal Reserve in the United States, intervened to provide liquidity and stabilize financial markets. These actions helped prevent a deeper and prolonged economic downturn.

The long-term effects of this crisis were:

- **Market reforms.** The Black Monday crash prompted reforms in financial markets, including the implementation of circuit breakers to halt trading during extreme volatility and tighter regulation of program trading.

- **Lessons learned.** It underscored the risks of speculative bubbles and the importance of market stability measures, influencing risk management practices in financial institutions and investment strategies.

Black Monday serves as a critical reminder of the volatility inherent in financial markets and the potential for rapid and severe downturns, prompting ongoing efforts to enhance market resilience and stability.

## The Asian Financial Crisis (1997)

The Asian Financial Crisis started in Thailand and quickly spread to neighboring countries. It was caused by a combination of excessive borrowing, risky investments and lack of confidence in the financial systems. Currencies devalued, stock markets crashed, and economies suffered deep recessions. The crisis had lasting effects on the economic policies and development strategies of the affected countries.

The crisis began with **currency devaluations** in Thailand (Baht) in July 1997, triggered by speculative attacks and unsustainable fixed exchange rates. Financial institutions and corporations in many Asian countries had borrowed heavily in foreign currencies, often to finance ambitious infrastructure projects and real estate ventures. When local currencies depreciated, these debts became increasingly difficult to repay. Weaknesses in financial and corporate governance, combined with external factors such as rising interest rates in the United States and declining export demand, exacerbated economic vulnerabilities.

A summary of the crisis impacts are listed below:

- **Economic contraction**. The crisis led to severe economic contractions in affected countries, with sharp declines in GDP growth rates and widespread recessionary conditions.

- **Currency and stock market turmoil**. Currency values plummeted, stock markets crashed, and foreign investors withdrew capital from the region, increasing financial instability.

- **Banking sector distress.** Many financial institutions faced insolvency due to non-performing loans and capital flight, necessitating government interventions and restructuring efforts.

- **Social and political unrest.** The economic downturn fueled social unrest and political instability in some countries, leading to protests and political transitions.

Government policies were put in place as a response to the crisis, such as:

- **IMF bailouts and structural adjustments.** The International Monetary Fund (IMF) provided financial assistance packages to affected countries in exchange for implementing structural reforms. These reforms included fiscal austerity measures, financial sector reforms and restructuring of corporate debts.

- **Currency interventions.** Central banks intervened in currency markets to stabilize exchange rates and restore investor confidence.

- **Reform and recovery efforts.** Governments implemented measures to strengthen financial regulations, improve transparency and diversify their economies to reduce dependency on volatile capital inflows.

The crisis prompted **reforms** aimed at enhancing financial stability, including **strengthening banking regulations**, improving corporate governance standards and developing regional financial cooperation mechanisms.

Countries affected by the crisis **diversified their economies** away from over-reliance on exports and foreign capital inflows, focusing on promoting domestic consumption and investment.

Efforts towards **regional economic integration** and cooperation, such as the ASEAN Economic Community (AEC), were accelerated to enhance economic resilience and stability.

The Asian Financial Crisis underscored the risks of financial liberalization without adequate safeguards, highlighting the importance of prudent macroeconomic management, sound financial regulation and policy coordination in preventing future crises.

## The Dot-Com Bubble Burst (2000)

The Dot-Com Bubble Burst, which occurred from 2000 to 2002, refers to the sharp decline in the stock prices of many internet-based companies in the United States and globally. It was a significant financial event characterized by the rapid rise and subsequent collapse of internet-related stocks. It highlighted the risks of speculative investing and underscored the importance of sound investment principles and market discipline in sustaining long-term economic growth and stability.

The most appointed causes are:

- **Speculative investment.** During the late 1990s, there was a frenzy of speculative investment in internet-based companies, fueled by the rapid growth of the internet and expectations of revolutionary technological advancements.

- **Overvaluation**. Many dot-com companies were valued based on potential rather than actual profits or sustainable business models. Investors poured funds into these companies, bidding up stock prices to unsustainable levels.

- **High risk appetite**. The prevailing sentiment among investors was one of optimism and willingness to overlook traditional valuation metrics in favor of growth potential.

Starting in early 2000, the stock prices of many dot-com companies began to decline sharply as investors reassessed the viability and profitability of these businesses. Numerous dot-com companies went bankrupt or were forced to merge as funding dried up and investor sentiment turned negative. This led to significant job losses and a contraction in the tech sector.

The bursting of the dot-com bubble caused a significant downturn in the technology sector, affecting not only internet companies but also telecommunications and related industries.

Many investors incurred **substantial losses** as stock prices plummeted, eroding market wealth and retirement savings.

The decline in the technology sector contributed to an **economic slowdown** in the United States and other countries, as tech-related investments and consumer spending contracted.

The bursting of the bubble prompted a reassessment of investment strategies, with a renewed focus on profitability and sustainable business models rather than speculative growth.

In response, governments and central banks implemented monetary and fiscal policies to stimulate economic growth and stabilize financial markets during the downturn.

The dot-com bubble and its aftermath led to a shift in investor behavior, with greater scrutiny of technology investments and a focus on fundamental financial metrics.

Despite the crash, the internet and technology sectors continued to innovate and evolve, laying the groundwork for future advancements in e-commerce, social media, and digital services.

The Securities and Exchange Commission (SEC) and other regulatory bodies implemented reforms to enhance transparency, corporate governance, and investor protections in response to the excesses of the dot-com era.

## The 2008 Global Financial Crisis

Another significant example is the 2008 Global Financial Crisis, triggered by the collapse of the housing bubble in the United States. Financial institutions had heavily invested in subprime mortgages, which defaulted when the housing market crashed. This led to the failure of major banks and financial institutions, prompting government bailouts and a severe global recession. Unemployment rates spiked, housing markets plummeted and many people faced foreclosures and financial ruin.

The events triggering this crisis were:

- **Housing market collapse.** The crisis began with the bursting of the U.S. housing bubble, fueled by excessive subprime mortgage lending and securitization of these risky loans.

- **Financial innovation and complexity**. Financial institutions engaged in the creation and trading of complex financial derivatives tied to mortgage-backed securities (MBS), which spread risk throughout the global financial system.

- **Credit crunch.** As housing prices declined and mortgage defaults surged, financial institutions faced substantial losses and liquidity problems, leading to a credit crunch and freezing of interbank lending.

- **Global contagion.** The interconnectedness of global financial markets meant that the crisis quickly spread to other countries and regions, causing widespread economic turmoil.

Major financial institutions, including Lehman Brothers, Bear Stearns and AIG, **collapsed** or required government **bailouts** to prevent systemic financial collapse.

Stock markets worldwide experienced sharp declines, eroding investor wealth and retirement savings. The crisis precipitated a severe global economic downturn, characterized by contracting GDP, rising unemployment and reduced consumer and business confidence.

Many homeowners faced foreclosure as housing prices plummeted, exacerbating the economic hardship for individuals and families.

Governments and central banks implemented unprecedented monetary and fiscal measures to stabilize financial markets, provide liquidity to banks and stimulate economic growth. These included interest rate cuts, bank rescues and stimulus packages.

The crisis prompted significant **regulatory reforms** aimed at enhancing financial stability, including the Dodd-Frank Wall Street Reform and Consumer Protection Act in the United States and Basel III regulations internationally. It also accelerated shifts in **global economic power and trade dynamics**, with emerging markets gaining relative importance. Besides that, the crisis eroded public trust in financial institutions and regulators, leading to calls for greater transparency, accountability and ethical practices in finance.

Despite recovery efforts, the effects of the 2008 Global Financial Crisis continue to resonate, influencing economic policies, financial sector practices and global economic resilience measures.

The 2008 Global Financial Crisis was a pivotal event that reshaped the global financial landscape, highlighting vulnerabilities in financial markets and prompting reforms to mitigate future crises while underscoring the importance of prudent risk management and regulatory oversight.

## The Importance of Preparation

Understanding financial crises and their impacts is relevant for several reasons:

- **Personal financial security.** Knowing how financial crises occur can help you **take proactive steps** to safeguard your finances. This includes building an emergency fund, diversifying your investments and managing debt wisely.

- **Economic stability.** On a broader scale, understanding financial crises can contribute to economic stability. Policymakers and financial institutions can develop better regulations and strategies to prevent or mitigate the effects of future crises.

- **Informed decision-making.** Knowledge of financial crises allows you to make informed decisions about your financial future. Whether it's investing, saving or planning for retirement, being aware of potential risks helps you prepare more effectively.

- **Psychological preparedness.** Financial crises can be stressful and overwhelming. Being prepared mentally and emotionally can help you navigate the challenges with greater resilience and confidence.

Financial crises are complex events with far-reaching impacts. By understanding their causes and effects, you can better prepare yourself and your finances for potential downturns. Historical examples like the Great Depression and the 2008 Global Financial Crisis highlight the importance of being vigilant and proactive. Preparation not only helps you protect your financial well-being but also contributes to broader economic stability.

In the following chapters, we'll explore practical steps you can take to safeguard your finances and build resilience against future financial crises.

# Chapter Two: Assessing Your Current Financial Health

Understanding your current financial health is an essential step in preparing for any financial crisis. It involves evaluating your income, expenses, and debts, understanding your net worth and creating a personal financial statement. By taking these steps, you can gain a clear picture of your financial situation and make informed decisions to protect your financial future.

## Evaluating Your Income, Expenses, and Debts

**Income:** Start by evaluating your income. This includes all sources of money you receive regularly, such as your salary, bonuses, freelance work, rental income and any other sources. Make a list of your income sources and their respective amounts. Knowing your total income helps you understand what you have to work with each month.

**Expenses:** Next, assess your expenses. Track all your spending for at least three months to get an accurate picture of where your money goes. Categorize your expenses into fixed (e.g., rent or mortgage, utilities, insurance) and variable (e.g., groceries, entertainment, dining out). This exercise will help you identify areas where you might be able to cut back if needed.

**Debts:** Finally, list all your debts, including credit cards, student loans, car loans and mortgages. Note the outstanding balance, interest rate and monthly payment for each debt. Understanding your debt load is important in order to create a plan to manage and reduce it.

## Understanding Your Net Worth

Your net worth is a snapshot of your financial health. It's calculated by subtracting your total liabilities (debts) from your total assets (what you own). Here is how to calculate it:

1. **List your assets**: Include everything you own that has value. This might include your home, car, savings accounts, retirement accounts, investments and personal property (e.g., jewelry, electronics, etc.).

2. **List your liabilities**: Include all your debts and financial obligations.

3. **Calculate net worth**: Subtract the total liabilities from the total assets. The result is your net worth.

A positive net worth means you own more than you owe, while a negative net worth means you owe more than you own. Understanding your net worth helps you see the big picture of your financial situation and track your progress over time.

## Creating a Personal Financial Statement

A personal financial statement is a document that outlines your financial position at a given point in time. It includes details about your income, expenses, assets and liabilities. Creating a personal financial statement can help you stay organized and make it easier to monitor your financial health. Here is how to create one:

- **Income statement**: List all sources of income and their amounts. Total these to get your monthly income.

- **Expense statement**: List all your monthly expenses, both fixed and variable. Total these to get your monthly expenses.

- **Balance sheet**:
  - **Assets**: List all your assets and their values. Total these to get your total assets.
  - **Liabilities**: List all your liabilities and their amounts. Total these to get your total liabilities.

- **Net worth calculation**: Subtract your total liabilities from your total assets to determine your net worth.

For more information about Personal Financial Statements and templates, checkout this resource: https://eforms.com/personal-financial-statement/.

## The Importance of Regular Financial Assessments

Regularly assessing your financial health is helpful especially when preparing for potential financial crises. By staying aware of your income, expenses, debts and net worth, you can:

- Identify areas where you can save money
- Develop strategies to pay down debt
- Make informed decisions about investments and savings
- Ensure you're on track to meet your financial goals

Assessing your current financial health is the foundation for preparing for any financial crisis. By evaluating your income, expenses and debts, understanding your net worth and creating a personal financial statement, you gain valuable insights into your financial situation. These steps empower you to make informed decisions and take proactive measures to safeguard your financial future.

In the next chapter, we'll explore how to build a robust emergency fund to protect yourself against unexpected financial challenges.

# Chapter Three: Diversifying Your Income Streams

In times of financial uncertainty, having multiple income streams can provide a safety net that protects you from economic downturns. Diversifying your income isn't just about boosting your earnings; it's about creating a more resilient financial foundation. In this chapter, we'll explore the benefits of having multiple income sources, ideas for side hustles and passive income, and the difference between long-term and short-term income diversification.

## The Benefits of Multiple Income Sources

### Financial Stability

Financial stability is a cornerstone of personal well-being and economic security, encompassing the ability to manage resources effectively, withstand financial shocks and achieve long-term financial goals. In times marked by economic uncertainties and frequent market fluctuations, maintaining financial stability has never been more critical.

At its core, financial stability means having a reliable income stream and a well-structured plan for managing expenses. A stable income allows individuals to meet their daily needs, save for the future and invest in opportunities for growth. It provides the foundation upon which other elements of financial stability are built, such as budgeting, saving, and investing. A well-structured budget ensures that spending aligns with income, preventing debt accumulation and enabling systematic savings.

One of the primary benefits of having multiple income streams is increased financial stability. Relying on a single source of income can be risky, especially if that source is jeopardized by job loss, industry downturns or other unforeseen events. Multiple income streams can cushion the blow if one source dries up, ensuring that you still have money coming in.

Additional income can accelerate your savings goals and provide more opportunities for investment. Whether you're saving for a down payment on a house, building an emergency fund or investing for retirement, having extra income can help you reach your financial goals faster.

Diversifying your income often involves learning new skills or pursuing different interests. This not only enriches your personal and professional life but also makes you more adaptable and marketable in the job market. The more skills and experience you have, the more opportunities you'll find.

## Side Hustles and Passive Income

### Side Hustles

Side hustles refer to additional income-generating activities that individuals pursue alongside their primary job or main source of income. These activities are typically flexible, allowing people to earn extra money outside of their regular working hours. Side hustles can range from freelance work and online gigs to small businesses or creative endeavors.

Side hustles are typically part-time activities that individuals engage in outside of their primary employment. They offer flexibility in terms of schedule and location, allowing people to work around their main job or other commitments. They also encompass a wide range of opportunities, from online platforms and freelancing to selling products or providing services.

Here are some side hustle ideas:

- **Freelancing**: Offer your skills in writing, graphic design, web development, or consulting on platforms like Upwork or Fiverr.

- **Ride-sharing or delivery services**: Drive for companies like Uber, Lyft, DoorDash or Postmates in your free time.

- **Tutoring or teaching**: Provide tutoring services or teach online classes through websites like VIPKid or Teachable.

- **Handmade crafts**: Sell handmade crafts or vintage items on Etsy.

- **Pet sitting or dog walking**: Offer pet care services through apps like Rover.

### Passive Income

Passive income refers to earnings derived from sources that require minimal effort or active involvement once set up. Unlike active income, which is earned through direct participation in a trade or business, passive income typically continues to generate revenue with little ongoing effort.

Setting up passive income streams often requires upfront effort, investment or skill development. Depending on the source, passive income may involve financial risks, market fluctuations or regulatory considerations. Income generated passively may be subject to different tax treatments compared to active income, so it's good to understand tax implications.

The main points of passive income are:

**Limited active involvement:** Passive income streams often require upfront effort or investment but can generate returns with minimal ongoing participation.

**Scalability**: Many passive income sources can be scaled up to increase earnings without proportionally increasing effort.

**Diverse sources**: Passive income can come from various sources such as investments, rental properties, royalties and certain types of businesses or partnerships.

Examples:

- **Real estate investing.** Purchase rental properties or invest in real estate crowdfunding platforms like Fundrise.

- **Dividend stocks.** Invest in dividend-paying stocks or exchange-traded funds (ETFs) to earn regular income from dividends.

- **Peer-to-peer lending.** Lend money through peer-to-peer lending platforms like LendingClub, earning interest on your loans.

- **Create digital products.** Develop e-books, online courses, or stock photos that can be sold repeatedly on platforms like Amazon or Udemy.

- **Royalties.** Payments received for the use of intellectual property, such as copyrights on books, music or patents.

- **Investment income.** Profits generated from investments in stocks, mutual funds, exchange-traded funds (ETFs), or real estate investment trusts (REITs).

- **Affiliate marketing.** Promote products or services on your blog or social media and earn commissions for sales through your affiliate links.

## Long-term vs. Short-term Income Diversification

### Short-term Income Diversification

Short-term income diversification focuses on generating immediate additional income. Side hustles are a prime example of this, as they can quickly supplement your primary income. While these may not always be sustainable in the long term, they can provide essential support during financial crises or when you need extra cash.

Benefits of short-term income diversification include:

- Immediate financial relief
- Flexibility to adapt to changing needs
- Opportunity to explore different income-generating activities

### Long-term Income Diversification

Long-term income diversification involves building income streams that can provide financial security over the years. This includes investments, real estate and passive income sources that grow over time. While these require more planning and initial effort, they offer significant benefits in terms of stability and growth.

Benefits of long-term income diversification include:

- Sustainable and reliable income sources
- Potential for significant wealth accumulation
- Reduced reliance on a single income source

Diversifying your income streams is a powerful strategy for building financial resilience and stability. Whether through short-term side hustles or long-term investments and passive income, having multiple sources of income can protect you from economic downturns and help you achieve your financial goals. By exploring different opportunities and finding what works best for you, you can create a robust financial foundation that withstands the test of time.

In the next chapter, we'll delve into smart investing during uncertain times, providing strategies to help you navigate volatile markets and secure your financial future.

# Chapter Four: Smart Investing During Uncertain Times

Investing during uncertain times can feel daunting, but with the right strategies, you can navigate volatile markets and protect your financial future. In this chapter, we'll explore effective investment strategies for volatile markets, the importance of diversifying your investment portfolio and the role of safe haven assets.

## Investment Strategies for Volatile Markets

### Stay Calm and Avoid Panic Selling

Market volatility can trigger emotional responses, leading to panic selling, where investors hastily liquidate their holdings at a loss, putting in risk their long-term financial goals. However, reacting impulsively to market swings can result in significant losses. Instead, focus on your long-term investment goals and avoid making decisions based on short-term market fluctuations.

One of the most effective ways to avoid panic selling is to maintain a long-term perspective. It's essential to remember that markets have historically rebounded from downturns, and short-term volatility is often just a blip on the radar in the grand scheme of a long-term investment strategy. By focusing on long-term goals and the overall growth potential of investments, investors can resist the urge to sell in a panic when markets dip.

Emotional control is perhaps the most challenging yet vital aspect of avoiding panic selling. Markets are influenced by a myriad of factors, many of which are beyond an individual investor's control. Accepting this and focusing on what can be controlled — such as asset allocation, risk tolerance and investment strategy — can reduce anxiety.

## Dollar-Cost Averaging

Dollar-cost averaging (DCA) is an investment strategy where you consistently invest a fixed amount of money at regular intervals, regardless of market conditions. This approach reduces the impact of market volatility by spreading your investments over time, potentially lowering the average cost of your investments.

Investors commit to investing a fixed amount of money at scheduled intervals, such as weekly, monthly or quarterly. With each investment interval, the investor buys more shares when prices are lower and fewer shares when prices are higher. This results in an average purchase price over time. Many investors automate dollar-cost averaging through automatic investment plans offered by brokerage firms or mutual fund companies.

**Key principles:**

**Mitigating market-timing risks.** Instead of trying to time the market to buy at the lowest price, dollar-cost averaging spreads out purchases over time, reducing the impact of short-term market fluctuations.

**Disciplined investing.** DCA encourages disciplined investing by committing to a regular investment schedule, regardless of market conditions or emotional reactions to market volatility.

**Potential benefits.** Over the long term, dollar-cost averaging can result in a lower average cost per share compared to investing a lump sum at a single point in time, especially in volatile markets.

**Example**:

Suppose an investor decides to invest $500 per month in a particular stock or mutual fund through a dollar-cost averaging strategy. In month 1, the stock price is $50 per share, so the investor buys 10 shares. In month 2, the price drops to $40 per share, allowing the investor to buy 12.5 shares. In month 3, the price rises to $60 per share, resulting in the purchase of 8.3 shares.

Over time, the investor accumulates shares at varying prices, leading to an average cost per share that reflects a blend of higher and lower purchase prices.

## Focus on Quality Investments

During volatile times, it's important to focus on high-quality investments with strong fundamentals. While market trends and news headlines often sway investor sentiment, focusing on the underlying strength of an investment can provide a more reliable path to long-term success.

First and foremost, understanding the business model of the company you're investing in is necessary. A strong business model is one that is sustainable, scalable and has a competitive edge in the market. Look for companies with a clear value proposition, a solid customer base and a strategic plan for growth. Companies that operate in industries with high barriers to entry or possess unique technologies or products often have a significant advantage over their competitors.

Next, examine the company's financial health by analyzing its financial statements. Key documents include the income statement, balance sheet and cash flow statement. The income statement reveals the company's profitability by detailing revenue, expenses and net income. A consistently profitable company with growing revenue and controlled expenses is typically a good sign. The balance sheet provides a snapshot of the company's assets, liabilities and shareholder equity. A strong balance sheet with a healthy ratio of assets to liabilities indicates financial stability.

Lastly, the cash flow statement shows how well the company generates cash to fund operations, pay debts and invest in growth. Positive and increasing cash flow from operations is a strong indicator of financial health.

Evaluating the company's earnings is another critical step. Look at the earnings per share (EPS), which measures the company's profitability on a per-share basis. Consistently growing EPS indicates that the company is effectively managing its resources and expanding its profitability. Additionally, consider the price-to-earnings (P/E) ratio, which compares the current share price to its per-share earnings. A lower P/E ratio compared to industry peers can indicate that the stock is undervalued, although it's important to consider the context and growth prospects.

Another key factor is the company's debt levels. High-quality investments typically have manageable levels of debt. The debt-to-equity (D/E) ratio, which compares a company's total liabilities to its shareholder equity, can provide insights into the company's leverage. A lower D/E ratio suggests that the company is not overly reliant on debt to finance its operations, reducing the risk of financial distress during economic downturns.

Look for companies with solid balance sheets, consistent earnings and a history of weathering economic downturns. Quality investments are more likely to recover from market downturns and provide long-term growth.

## Maintain a Long-Term Perspective

Investing is a long-term endeavor. Moreover, market volatility is a normal part of the investment journey. Historically, markets have rebounded from downturns and continued to grow. By maintaining a long-term perspective, you can ride out short-term volatility and benefit from the market's overall upward trend.

## Diversifying Your Investment Portfolio

### The Importance of Diversification

When markets become volatile and economic conditions worsen, a well-diversified portfolio can provide a buffer against severe losses, helping investors navigate through turbulent times with greater confidence and stability. The importance of diversification becomes particularly evident in the face of a financial crisis, where the interconnectedness of global markets can amplify the impact of economic downturns.

Diversification involves spreading your investments across various asset classes, sectors and geographic regions to reduce risk.

This strategy reduces the risk associated with any single investment by ensuring that the overall performance of the portfolio is not overly dependent on one particular asset or market. By holding a mix of assets such as stocks, bonds, real estate and commodities, investors can minimize the impact of poor performance in any single investment, thereby enhancing the portfolio's resilience.

One of the primary benefits of diversification is the reduction of unsystematic risk, which is the risk associated with individual investments. For instance, a company-specific event, such as a scandal or a product failure, can significantly affect the stock price of that company. However, if an investor holds a diversified portfolio of stocks across different industries, the negative impact of one company's poor performance can be offset by the positive performance of other investments. This balance helps stabilize the overall portfolio returns.

During a financial crisis, certain asset classes and sectors may be more adversely affected than others. For example, in the 2008 Global Financial Crisis, the financial sector was particularly hard hit due to the collapse of major banks and financial institutions. Investors who had a significant portion of their portfolios in financial stocks experienced substantial losses. However, those with diversified portfolios that included assets less correlated with the financial sector, such as government bonds or precious metals, were better protected against the downturn.

Diversification also helps in maintaining liquidity during financial crises. Some assets can be quickly and easily converted into cash without significantly affecting their value, while others may be less liquid. Having a mix of liquid and illiquid assets ensures that investors have access to funds when needed, without being forced to sell investments at a loss during market downturns.

While diversification is not a guarantee against loss, it is a proven strategy for managing risk and enhancing the potential for long-term returns. It requires careful planning and regular review to ensure that the portfolio remains aligned with the investor's goals and risk tolerance. In times of financial crisis, diversification provides the dual benefits of risk reduction and potential capital preservation, allowing investors to weather the storm more effectively.

## Asset Allocation

Asset allocation is the process of dividing your investment portfolio among different asset categories, such as stocks, bonds, and cash. The right asset allocation depends on your risk tolerance, time horizon, and financial goals.

- **Stocks**: Provide growth potential but come with higher volatility.
- **Bonds**: Offer stability and regular income but typically have lower returns than stocks.
- **Cash**: Provides liquidity and safety but offers minimal returns.

A balanced portfolio might include a mix of these asset classes to achieve both growth and stability.

## Sector and Geographic Diversification

In addition to diversifying by asset class, consider spreading your investments across different sectors (e.g., technology, healthcare, finance) and geographic regions (e.g., domestic, international, emerging markets). This approach can further reduce risk by ensuring that your investments are not overly concentrated in any one area.

Economic conditions and market performance can vary significantly across different countries and regions. By investing in a range of international markets, investors can reduce the risk associated with economic downturns in any single country. For instance, while one country's economy may be in recession, another's may be experiencing growth. Geographic diversification allows investors to capitalize on global opportunities and reduce the impact of regional economic issues.

# Safe Haven Assets and Their Role

## What Are Safe Haven Assets?

During financial crises, safe-haven assets such as gold often appreciate in value as investors seek refuge from the turmoil in equity markets. By balancing investments across different asset classes, investors can achieve a more stable and predictable portfolio performance.

These safe haven assets are investments that investors flock to during times of economic uncertainty. These assets are considered relatively stable and tend to retain or increase in value when other investments, such as stocks or higher-risk assets, experience significant declines. Safe haven assets are sought after for their perceived reliability and ability to preserve capital in turbulent market conditions.

While safe haven assets provide stability, they may not offer high returns compared to riskier investments during periods of economic expansion.

Timing the entry and exit from safe haven assets requires consideration of market cycles and economic indicators.

The main characteristics of safe haven assets are:

- **Low volatility.** Safe haven assets typically exhibit lower price volatility compared to riskier assets like stocks or commodities.

- **Liquidity.** They are readily convertible to cash without significant price discounts, ensuring investors can access funds quickly if needed.

- **Perceived stability.** Safe haven assets are perceived to retain value or increase in value during economic downturns or periods of market stress.

Common safe haven assets include:

- **Gold.** Gold is historically one of the most popular safe haven assets. It is viewed as a store of value and a hedge against inflation and currency fluctuations. During times of economic uncertainty, demand for gold tends to increase, driving up its price.

- **Cash and cash equivalents.** Cash in **stable** currencies is considered a safe haven asset. Investors may hold cash to maintain liquidity and preserve capital during volatile market periods.

- **High-quality bonds**. Bonds issued by stable governments or high-quality corporate bonds with strong credit ratings are also considered safe haven assets. These bonds provide regular interest payments and are less likely to default compared to lower-rated bonds.

- **Defensive stocks**. Some stocks in sectors that are less sensitive to economic cycles, such as utilities, consumer staples and healthcare, may be considered safe haven investments. These stocks tend to have stable earnings and dividends, making them attractive during market downturns.

- **Precious metals**: Besides gold, other precious metals like silver, platinum and palladium are sometimes considered safe haven assets due to their scarcity, industrial uses and store of value properties.

Safe haven assets should not dominate your portfolio. Instead, consider allocating a portion of your investments to this type of assets to balance risk and return. The right allocation depends on your risk tolerance and investment goals.

Smart investing during uncertain times requires a combination of strategies that focus on long-term goals, quality investments, diversification, and the incorporation of safe haven assets. By staying calm and avoiding panic selling, using dollar-cost averaging and maintaining a diversified portfolio, you can navigate volatile markets more effectively.

In the next chapter, we will explore managing debt effectively, providing practical tips and strategies to reduce and manage your debt load during financial crises.

# Chapter Five: Managing Debt Effectively

Debt can be a significant burden, especially during a financial crisis. Effective debt management is an important factor to maintain financial stability and reduce stress. In this chapter, we will cover how to prioritize and pay off high-interest debts, explore debt consolidation options and discuss the importance of using credit responsibly.

## Prioritizing and Paying Off High-Interest Debts

### Assess Your Debt Situation

The first step in managing debt effectively is to understand your current debt situation. Make a list of all your debts, including:

- Credit cards
- Personal loans
- Student loans
- Car loans
- Mortgages

For each debt, note the outstanding balance, interest rate and minimum monthly payment.
Prioritizing high-interest debt is a critical strategy. High-interest debts, such as credit card balances, can quickly escalate if not addressed promptly. Focus on paying down these debts first, as they

cost you more money in the long run. One effective approach is the avalanche method.

## The Debt Avalanche Method

The avalanche method focuses on paying off debts with the highest interest rates first. Here is how it works:

1. **List your debts by interest rate**. Arrange your debts from highest to lowest interest rate.
2. **Make minimum payments.** Continue making minimum payments on all your debts.
3. **Allocate extra payments.** Direct any extra money towards the debt with the highest interest rate.
4. **Repeat.** Once the highest-interest debt is paid off, move to the next one on your list.

By prioritizing high-interest debts, you reduce the total amount of interest you pay over time, helping you become debt-free faster.

## The Debt Snowball Method

Another popular strategy is the snowball method. This involves paying off the smallest debts first, regardless of interest rate, to gain a psychological boost from eliminating debts. While this method may not save as much on interest, the sense of accomplishment can be motivating and help you stay committed to your debt repayment plan. It focuses on paying off the smallest debts first:

1. **List your debts by balance.** Arrange your debts from smallest to largest balance.
2. **Make minimum payments**. Continue making minimum payments on all your debts.
3. **Allocate extra payments.** Direct any extra money towards the smallest debt.
4. **Repeat.** Once the smallest debt is paid off, move to the next one on your list.

## Debt Consolidation Options

Debt consolidation involves combining multiple debts into a single loan or payment. This can simplify your payments and potentially lower your interest rates. Here are some common debt consolidation options:

- **Balance transfer credit cards.** A balance transfer credit card allows you to transfer existing credit card balances to a new card with a lower interest rate, often with an introductory 0% APR period. This can help you pay off your debt faster without accruing additional interest. However, **be mindful of balance transfer fees** and ensure you can **pay off the balance before the introductory period ends**.

- **Personal Loans.** A personal loan can be used to consolidate multiple debts into a single loan with a fixed interest rate and monthly payment. This can make managing your debt easier and potentially lower your overall interest rate. Shop around for the best loan terms and ensure you understand the fees and repayment terms.

- **Home equity loans or HELOCs.** If you own a home, you might consider a home equity loan or home equity line of credit (HELOC) to consolidate debt. These options often have lower interest rates compared to credit cards or personal loans. However, they use your home as collateral, meaning you risk losing your home if you cannot make the payments.

## Using Credit Responsibly

Responsible credit usage is crucial for maintaining a healthy financial situation. Here are some tips for using credit wisely:

- **Keep credit card balances low.** Aim to use less than 30% of your available credit limit.

- **Pay bills on time.** Timely payments help maintain a good credit score and avoid late fees.

- **Avoid Unnecessary Debt.** Only use credit for necessary expenses and avoid impulse purchases.

### Build an Emergency Fund

An emergency fund can prevent you from relying on credit cards for unexpected expenses. Aim to save three to six months' worth of living expenses in an easily accessible account. This fund can provide a financial cushion during a crisis, helping you avoid accumulating more debt.

### Regularly Review Your Credit Report

Regularly reviewing your credit report can help you stay on top of your credit health and catch any errors or signs of identity theft.

Managing debt effectively is essential for financial stability, especially during a financial crisis. By prioritizing and paying off high-interest debts, exploring debt consolidation options and using credit responsibly, you can reduce your debt burden and improve your financial health.

In the next chapter, let us explore strategies for protecting your assets, including the importance of insurance and ensuring you have the proper coverage to safeguard your financial future.

# Chapter Six: Protecting Your Assets

In the midst of a financial crisis, safeguarding your assets becomes paramount. Protecting your assets through proper insurance coverage can shield you from unexpected financial shocks and ensure long-term stability. In this chapter, we will discuss the importance of insurance, types of insurance to consider and how to ensure you have proper coverage.

## The Importance of Insurance

Insurance acts as a safety net, providing financial protection against unforeseen events. Whether it's health issues, accidents, natural disasters or liability claims, having the right insurance can prevent these situations from depleting your savings or plunging you into debt.

Insurance provides financial security by covering significant expenses that could otherwise drain your resources. For instance, health insurance can cover medical bills, while homeowners insurance can pay for repairs after a natural disaster. Without insurance, such unexpected costs could severely impact your financial health.

Knowing that you are protected against potential risks offers peace of mind. You can focus on other aspects of your life without constantly worrying about financial ruin due to unforeseen events. **This mental reassurance is invaluable**, especially during uncertain times.

Certain types of insurance, like liability insurance, protect you from legal claims. If you are sued for causing injury or damage, liability insurance can cover legal fees and settlements, safeguarding your assets from being seized to pay for these costs.

## Types of Insurance to Consider

There are various types of insurance policies designed to protect different aspects of your life and assets. Here are some essential types to consider:

- **Health Insurance.** Health insurance is crucial for covering medical expenses, from routine check-ups to major surgeries. It ensures you receive necessary medical care without worrying about the high costs. Options include employer-provided plans, individual policies and government programs.

- **Homeowners/renters insurance.** Homeowners insurance protects your home and personal property against damage or loss due to events like fire, theft or natural disasters. It also provides liability coverage if someone is injured on your property. Renters insurance offers similar protection for those who lease their homes, covering personal belongings and liability.

- **Auto insurance.** Auto insurance is mandatory in most places and covers costs related to car accidents, including property damage, medical expenses, and liability for injuries to others. Comprehensive and collision coverage can also protect against non-accident-related damage, such as theft or vandalism.

- **Life insurance.** Life insurance provides financial support to your beneficiaries in the event of your death. It can help cover funeral expenses, pay off debts and provide income replacement for your family. There are various types of life insurance, including term life, whole life and universal life policies.

- **Disability insurance.** Disability insurance replaces a portion of your income if you are unable to work due to illness or injury. Short-term disability covers temporary disabilities, while long-term disability provides benefits for more extended periods, ensuring you can meet your financial obligations even if you can't work.

- **Liability insurance.** Liability insurance protects you from legal claims if you are held responsible for causing injury or damage to someone else. It includes personal liability coverage, often part of homeowners or renters insurance and umbrella policies that offer additional liability protection beyond standard policy limits.

## Ensuring Proper Coverage

Having insurance is beneficial, but it's equally important to ensure you have the right coverage to adequately protect your assets.

Here are steps to ensure proper coverage:

- **Assess your needs.** Evaluate your assets, lifestyle and potential risks to determine the types and amounts of coverage you need. Consider factors like the value of your home and possessions, your income, dependents and any specific risks associated with your location or activities.

- **Compare policies.** Shop around and compare policies from different insurers. Look at coverage options, limits, exclusions and premiums to find the best fit for your needs and budget. Online comparison tools and consultations with insurance agents can help you make informed decisions.

- **Regularly review and update coverage.** Life circumstances change and your insurance needs may evolve over time. Regularly review your policies to ensure they still provide adequate coverage. Update your coverage if you experience significant life changes, such as buying a new home, getting married, having children or starting a new job.

- **Understand policy details.** Thoroughly read and understand the details of your insurance policies. Know what is covered, any exclusions, deductibles and the process for filing claims. Being well-informed about your policies ensures you can effectively use your coverage when needed.

Protecting your assets through proper insurance coverage is a fundamental aspect of financial planning, especially during a financial crisis. By understanding the importance of insurance, considering essential types of coverage and ensuring you have the right policies in place, you can safeguard your financial future against unexpected events.

In the next chapter, we will explore creating a financial contingency plan, providing strategies to prepare for and navigate potential financial crises with confidence.

# Chapter Seven: Cutting Costs and Budgeting Wisely

During a financial crisis, effective budgeting and cost-cutting strategies are very important. By identifying unnecessary expenses, creating a flexible budget and adopting frugal living habits, you can manage your finances more effectively. In this chapter, we will explore these strategies in detail to help you take control of your financial situation.

## Identifying and Eliminating Unnecessary Expenses

The first step to cutting costs is understanding where your money goes. Track all your expenses for a month, categorizing them into needs (essential) and wants (non-essential). This can be done using budgeting apps, spreadsheets or even a simple notebook.

Use technology to your advantage by leveraging budgeting apps or financial tracking tools. Many apps allow you to link your bank accounts and credit cards, automatically categorize transactions and generate reports on your spending habits. This automation can save time and provide real-time insights into where your money is going, making it easier to identify areas where you can reduce expenses. Knowing your spending habits is the key to identifying areas where you can cut back.

During a financial crisis, it's important to distinguish between essential and non-essential expenses. Focus on covering your basic needs, such as food, shelter, utilities and healthcare, before allocating funds to discretionary spending.

Communicate openly with family members or household members about financial priorities and budgeting goals. Collaborate on decision-making processes and encourage everyone to contribute to cost-saving measures. This shared responsibility fosters financial transparency and accountability, ensuring that everyone is working towards common financial objectives during challenging times.

Monthly subscriptions and memberships can add up quickly. Review all your subscriptions, such as streaming services, gym memberships, magazines and apps. Cancel those you rarely use or can live without. Consider sharing subscriptions with family or friends to reduce costs.

Utility bills can be a significant part of your monthly expenses but they can be reduced. Simple changes can lead to substantial savings:

- **Energy Efficiency**. Use energy-efficient appliances and light bulbs. Unplug electronics when not in use and consider a programmable thermostat.

- **Water Conservation**. Fix leaks, take shorter showers and use water-saving fixtures.

- **Shop Around**. Compare rates from different utility providers and switch to cheaper plans if available.

Consider negotiating with service providers or creditors to lower monthly payments or defer payments temporarily if necessary to alleviate financial strain.

Eating out and ordering takeout can be convenient but expensive. Try cooking more meals at home, planning your weekly menu and preparing meals in bulk. Bring lunch to work instead of buying it and treat dining out as an occasional treat rather than a regular habit.

## Creating a Flexible Budget

**Determine your income and expenses.** Start by listing all sources of income, including salary, side hustles and any other regular earnings. Then, list all your monthly expenses, both fixed (rent, mortgage, utilities) and variable (groceries, entertainment, transportation).

**Categorize and prioritize.** Categorize your expenses into needs and wants. Needs include essentials like housing, utilities, food, transportation and insurance. Wants are non-essential items like dining out, entertainment and luxury purchases. Prioritize your needs and allocate funds accordingly.

**Set realistic goals.** Set realistic financial goals, such as paying off debt, building an emergency fund or saving for a major purchase. These goals will help guide your budgeting decisions and keep you motivated.

**Monitor and adjust.** A budget is not set in stone. Monitor your spending regularly and compare it to your budget. Adjust your budget as needed to accommodate changes in income or unexpected expenses. Flexibility is key to maintaining a workable budget.

## Tips for Frugal Living

**Embrace minimalism.** Minimalism focuses on owning fewer possessions and prioritizing quality over quantity. By adopting a minimalist mindset, you can reduce clutter and save money by only buying what you truly need and value.

**DIY and homemade Solutions.** Doing things yourself can save a lot of money. Learn basic home maintenance, cooking and crafting skills. Make homemade gifts, clean with DIY solutions and repair items instead of replacing them.

**Shop Smart.** Be a savvy shopper to save money:

- **Buy in Bulk.** Purchase non-perishable items in bulk to save on unit costs.

- **Use Coupons and Discounts.** Look for coupons, discounts and cashback offers when shopping.

- **Thrift and secondhand.** Buy clothes, furniture and other items from thrift stores, consignment shops or online marketplaces.

**Plan and Prepare.** Planning ahead can prevent unnecessary spending:

- **Meal planning**: Plan your meals for the week, make a shopping list and stick to it to avoid impulse purchases.

- **Avoid impulse buys**: Implement a 24-hour rule for non-essential purchases. Wait a day before buying to see if you still want it.

- **Budget for fun**: Allocate a small portion of your budget for entertainment and leisure to avoid feeling deprived.

Cutting costs and budgeting wisely are essential skills for navigating a financial crisis. By identifying and eliminating unnecessary expenses, creating a flexible budget and adopting frugal living habits, you can take control of your finances and build a more resilient financial future.

The next chapter will explore building an emergency fund, provide practical tips and strategies to ensure you have a financial cushion to rely on during tough times.

# Chapter Eight: Staying Informed and Adapting

This chapter explores the importance of financial literacy, resources for staying updated on economic trends and how to adapt your financial plan as needed.

## The Importance of Financial Literacy

Financial literacy is the ability to understand and use various financial skills, including personal financial management, budgeting and investing. It equips you with the knowledge to make informed decisions about your money, reducing the risk of financial missteps.

With a strong foundation in financial literacy, you can make better decisions regarding spending, saving, investing and borrowing. This helps you avoid high-interest debt, choose appropriate investment options and create a robust financial plan that withstands economic uncertainties.

Financial literacy builds confidence in managing your finances. Understanding how different financial products work, knowing how to interpret financial news and being aware of economic trends empower you to take control of your financial future.

# Resources for Staying Updated on Economic Trends

**Financial news websites.** Reputable financial news websites provide up-to-date information on economic trends, market movements and financial advice. Some popular resources include:

- **Bloomberg**: Comprehensive coverage of global financial markets and economic news.

- **Reuters**: In-depth analysis of financial and economic developments.

- **CNBC**: Live updates on stock markets, economic news and personal finance tips.

**Financial blogs and podcasts.** Blogs and podcasts can offer unique insights and expert opinions on financial topics. Some recommended blogs and podcasts are:

- **The Motley Fool**: Investment advice and stock market analysis.
- **NPR's Planet Money**: Engaging stories about the economy and financial trends.
- **Mr. Money Mustache**: Practical advice on frugal living and financial independence.

**Government and institutional reports.** Government agencies and financial institutions regularly publish reports on economic conditions and forecasts. Key sources include:

- **Federal Reserve**: Reports on economic conditions, monetary policy, and financial stability.
- **Bureau of Economic Analysis (BEA)**: Data on GDP, personal income, and consumer spending.
- **International Monetary Fund (IMF)**: Global economic outlooks and financial stability reports.

**Educational Courses and Workshops.** Many organizations offer courses and workshops on financial literacy and economic trends.

These can be found online or through local community centers, universities and non-profits. Websites like Coursera and Khan Academy offer free or low-cost courses on various financial topics.

## Adapting Your Financial Plan as Needed

Your financial plan should be a living document that evolves with your circumstances and the broader economic environment. Regularly review your financial goals, income, expenses and investments to ensure they align with your current situation and future aspirations.

Flexibility is key to adapting your financial plan. Be open to adjusting your budget, reallocating investments or exploring new income sources as economic conditions change. This proactive approach helps you stay resilient during financial crises.

Having contingency plans in place can help you navigate financial uncertainties more smoothly. This might include:

- **Emergency fund**: Ensure you have a robust emergency fund to cover at least three to six months of living expenses.

- **Alternative income sources**: Identify potential side hustles or passive income streams that can provide financial support if your primary income is affected.

- **Debt management strategies**: Have a plan for managing and paying off debt, including understanding your options for debt consolidation or seeking professional financial advice if needed.

## Monitor Key Economic Indicators

There are indicators that provide insights into the health of the economy, potential risks and signals of impending financial turmoil. By monitoring these indicators, stakeholders can make informed decisions to protect assets, mitigate risks and navigate through turbulent economic periods.

Keep an eye on key economic indicators that can signal changes in the financial environment, such as:

**Gross Domestic Product (GDP).** GDP measures the total value of goods and services produced within a country over a specific period. A significant decline in GDP, especially over consecutive quarters (recession), can indicate economic contraction and potential recessionary conditions. A prolonged decline in GDP is often associated with reduced consumer spending, business investment and overall economic activity, signaling a weakening economy and potential financial instability.

**Unemployment rate.** The unemployment rate reflects the percentage of the labor force that is actively seeking employment but unable to find jobs. During a financial crisis, unemployment typically rises as businesses cut costs, reduce hiring or lay off workers to cope with economic challenges. High unemployment rates can lead to reduced consumer spending, increased loan defaults and economic hardship for individuals and families, raising financial instability.

**Stock market performance.** Stock market indices (such as the S&P 500 or Dow Jones Industrial Average, in the USA) provide insights into investor sentiment and market confidence. Sharp declines in stock prices over a short period, often referred to as a market correction or crash, can signal widespread concerns about economic growth, corporate profitability or financial system stability. A sustained bear market, characterized by prolonged declines in stock prices, may indicate broader economic weakness and potential systemic risks.

**Interest rates.** Central banks adjust interest rates to influence borrowing costs, inflation and economic growth. During a financial crisis, central banks may lower interest rates to stimulate economic activity, encourage borrowing and support financial markets. Conversely, rising interest rates, particularly if they increase rapidly or unexpectedly, can tighten financial conditions, constrain consumer spending and impact business investment, potentially exacerbating economic challenges.

**Consumer Confidence Index.** The Consumer Confidence Index (CCI) measures consumers' optimism about the economy's future outlook, job prospects and personal finances. A decline in consumer confidence during a financial crisis reflects heightened concerns about economic conditions, job security and income stability.

Reduced consumer confidence can lead to lower consumer spending, weaker retail sales and overall economic slowdown, contributing to financial instability.

**Corporate profits**. Corporate profits provide insights into the financial health and profitability of businesses. During a financial crisis, declining corporate profits, particularly across multiple sectors or industries, may signal reduced business activity, lower consumer demand and profitability challenges. Profit warnings or earnings downgrades from companies can impact investor sentiment, stock prices and market stability, highlighting potential economic vulnerabilities.

**Credit spreads and bond yields.** Credit spreads, which measure the difference in yields between corporate bonds and safer government bonds (such as Treasury bonds), provide insights into investor risk appetite and credit market conditions. Widening credit spreads during a financial crisis indicate increased investor aversion to risk, higher borrowing costs for businesses and potential liquidity challenges in credit markets. Rising bond yields, particularly for government bonds perceived as safe havens, may signal investor flight to quality amid economic uncertainty.

**Housing market indicators**. The housing market is closely watched as a barometer of economic health. During a financial crisis, declines in home sales, falling property prices and rising foreclosure rates may indicate weakening consumer confidence, reduced household wealth and financial distress among homeowners. Distressed housing market conditions can contribute to broader economic instability, impacting consumer spending, mortgage lending and financial sector health.

**Currency exchange rates**. Currency exchange rates reflect the relative strength of a country's currency compared to others. During a financial crisis, currency volatility, depreciation or sudden declines can signal investor concerns about economic fundamentals, fiscal policies or external shocks. Currency instability may impact trade flows, inflation expectations and global market sentiment, influencing economic stability and financial market performance.

**Government debt and fiscal policies.** Government debt levels and fiscal policies play a crucial role in addressing economic challenges during a financial crisis. High government debt burdens, fiscal deficits or unsustainable spending can strain public finances, limit policy options and erode investor confidence. Effective fiscal policies, such as stimulus measures or austerity measures, can impact economic recovery, market stability and long-term fiscal sustainability.

By staying informed about these indicators, you can make timely adjustments to your financial plan. Staying informed and adapting your financial plan is essential for successfully navigating financial crises. By enhancing your financial literacy, utilizing reliable resources to stay updated on economic trends, and being flexible with your financial strategies, you can build resilience and protect your financial future.

The next chapter will highlight the importance of planning for the long term.

# Chapter Nine: Planning for the Long Term

In the midst of a financial crisis, it's important not to lose sight of your long-term financial goals. Setting financial goals, planning for retirement and ensuring your estate is in order are essential steps to securing your financial future and protecting your legacy. This chapter will guide you through these processes, offering practical advice for navigating uncertain times.

## Setting Financial Goals

### Define Clear and Achievable Goals

Setting financial goals gives you a roadmap to follow and helps you stay focused on your long-term financial well-being. Begin by defining clear, specific and achievable goals. These might include:

- **Short-term goals**: Paying off credit card debt, building an emergency fund, saving for a vacation.
- **Medium-term goals**: Saving for a down payment on a house, funding a child's education, buying a car.
- **Long-term goals**: Saving for retirement, purchasing investment properties, leaving a financial legacy.

### Make Your Goals SMART

SMART goals are a framework for setting clear and achievable objectives. The acronym SMART stands for Specific, Measurable, Achievable, Relevant, and Time-bound. This framework helps individuals define and track progress toward their goals effectively. It provides clarity and focus, ensuring everyone understands what needs to be achieved and why it matters.

Ensure your financial goals are SMART. For example, instead of saying "save more money", set a goal like "save $5,000 for an emergency fund within 12 months."

SMART goals are:

- **Specific**: Goals should be clear, well-defined, and specific. They answer the questions: What do I want to accomplish? Why is this goal important? What resources or constraints are involved?

- **Measurable**: Goals should be quantifiable and include metrics or criteria for tracking progress. Measurable goals help assess whether the objective is being met and provide a way to gauge success.

- **Achievable**: Goals should be realistic and attainable given the resources, time frame and circumstances. They should stretch your abilities but remain within the realm of possibility.

- **Relevant**: Goals should align with broader objectives and be relevant to your overall vision or purpose. They should contribute to personal or organizational growth and be meaningful in the context of your priorities.

- **Time-bound**: Goals should have a specific timeframe or deadline for completion. This helps create a sense of urgency and focus, preventing goals from dragging on indefinitely.

## Break Down Your Goals

Breaking down your larger goals into smaller, manageable steps can make them less daunting and easier to achieve. For instance, if your goal is to save $5,000 in a year, plan to save about $417 per month or around $100 per week.

## Retirement Planning in Uncertain Times

**Understand Your Retirement Needs.** Estimating your retirement needs involves considering various factors such as your desired lifestyle, life expectancy, healthcare costs and inflation. Use retirement calculators and consult financial advisors to get a realistic picture of how much you'll need.

**Diversify Your Retirement Savings.** Diversification is key to mitigating risk, especially during uncertain times. Consider spreading your retirement savings across different types of accounts and investments, including:

- **Employer-sponsored retirement plans** (often include matching contributions).

- **Individual retirement accounts**.

- **Investment portfolios**: Stocks, bonds, mutual funds and ETFs can provide growth potential and income.

- **Real estate**: Investment properties can offer rental income and appreciation over time.

**Adjust your contributions.** Continue to contribute to your retirement savings, even in uncertain economic times and even if you need to adjust the amounts. If your income fluctuates, try to maintain at least a minimum contribution, and increase it when your financial situation improves.

**Reassess your risk tolerance.** Market volatility can impact your retirement investments. Regularly reassess your risk tolerance and adjust your investment strategy accordingly. As you approach retirement, consider shifting to more conservative investments to preserve your capital.

## Estate Planning and Protecting Your Legacy

**Create or Update Your Will.** A will is a fundamental component of estate planning. It ensures that your assets are distributed according to your wishes and can help avoid potential disputes among heirs. If you don't have a will, create one. If you do, review and update it regularly, especially after major life events like marriage, divorce or the birth of a child.

**Establish a Trust.** Trusts can offer greater control over how your assets are managed and distributed. They can also provide tax benefits and help avoid probate.

A trust is a legal arrangement in which one party, known as the trustor, settlor or grantor, transfers assets such as money, property or investments to another party known as the trustee. The trustee holds and manages these assets on behalf of a third party, known as the beneficiary or beneficiaries, according to the terms specified in the trust agreement. Trusts are commonly used for estate planning, asset protection and charitable purposes.

Common types of trusts include:

- **Revocable trust (living trust)**: A trust that can be altered, amended or revoked by the trustor during their lifetime. It becomes irrevocable upon the trustor's death and typically avoids probate for assets held within the trust.

- **Irrevocable trust**: A trust that cannot be modified or terminated by the trustor once it is established. It provides asset protection and may offer tax benefits, but requires careful consideration due to its permanence.

- **Testamentary trust**: A trust established through a will and takes effect upon the death of the trustor. It allows for control over the distribution of assets to beneficiaries after death.

- **Charitable trust**: A trust established for charitable purposes, with a designated charity or charitable cause as the beneficiary. It can provide tax advantages and support philanthropic goals.

- **Special needs trust**: A trust designed to provide for the ongoing care and financial support of a person with disabilities, while preserving their eligibility for government benefits.

- **Asset protection trust**: A trust created to shield assets from creditors or legal claims, typically established in jurisdictions with favorable asset protection laws.

**Designate beneficiaries.** Ensure that all your financial accounts, retirement plans and life insurance policies have up-to-date beneficiary designations. This ensures that these assets are transferred directly to your beneficiaries, bypassing probate.

**Plan for incapacity.** Prepare for the possibility of incapacity by setting up a durable power of attorney and healthcare proxy. These legal documents allow trusted individuals to make financial and medical decisions on your behalf if you are unable to do so.

Planning for the long term is a vital component of financial stability, especially during a financial crisis. By setting clear financial goals, diversifying and adjusting your retirement plans and ensuring your estate is properly managed, you can secure your financial future and protect your legacy.

In the next chapter, we will explore building a strong support network, including professional advisors, community resources, and personal relationships, to help you manage and overcome financial challenges.

# Chapter Ten: Psychological Preparedness

Managing your emotional and mental well-being during a financial crisis is just as crucial as managing your finances. This chapter explores strategies for coping with financial stress and anxiety, building resilience, maintaining a positive mindset and knowing when to seek professional financial advice.

## Coping with Financial Stress and Anxiety

**Recognize your stress triggers.** Financial stress can stem from various sources, such as job loss, debt, market volatility or unexpected expenses. Identify what triggers your stress to better manage its impact on your well-being.

**Practice stress-relief techniques.** Implementing stress-relief techniques can help alleviate financial anxiety:

- **Deep breathing**. Take slow, deep breaths to calm your mind and reduce stress levels.

- **Exercise**. Engage in physical activities like walking, yoga or jogging to release tension and boost mood.

- **Mindfulness and meditation.** Practice mindfulness techniques or meditation to center yourself and reduce anxiety.

- **Healthy lifestyle**: Maintain a balanced diet, get enough sleep and limit caffeine and alcohol intake, as they can exacerbate stress.

**Seek Emotional Support.** Talk to trusted friends and family members about your financial concerns. Sharing your feelings can provide emotional support and help you gain perspective on your situation.

## Building Resilience and a Positive Mindset

**Focus on What You Can Control.** While you may not control external economic factors, focus on what you can control, such as your budget, spending habits and savings goals. Taking proactive steps empowers you and reduces feelings of helplessness.

**Practice Gratitude.** Cultivating gratitude can shift your perspective and boost resilience. Each day, reflect on things you are grateful for, whether it's supportive relationships, good health or small achievements.

**Set Realistic Expectations.** Acknowledge that financial crises are temporary and often part of larger economic cycles. Setting realistic expectations can help you navigate uncertainties with greater resilience.

## Seeking Professional Financial Advice When Needed

If you're overwhelmed by financial decisions or unsure about your financial strategy, seek guidance from a professional financial advisor. They can provide expert advice tailored to your specific circumstances and goals.

Types of financial advisors that could help you:

- **Certified Financial Planner (CFP).** Offers comprehensive financial planning advice, including investments, retirement planning and estate planning.

- **Financial advisor.** Provides guidance on investment strategies and financial goals.

- **Credit counselor.** Helps with debt management and budgeting.

Professional financial advisors can:

- **Provide clarity.** Gain a clear understanding of your financial situation and options available to you.

- **Create a plan.** Develop a personalized financial plan aligned with your goals and risk tolerance.

- **Navigate complexity.** Receive guidance on complex financial matters, such as tax planning or investment diversification.

In order to choose the right advisor, look for those with relevant credentials and certifications, such as CFP or registered investment advisor (RIA). Also consider their experience in dealing with clients in similar financial situations. Understand their fee structure and ensure it aligns with your preferences (fee-only, commission-based or a combination).

Psychological preparedness is important to navigate financial crises with resilience and maintain a positive outlook. By coping with financial stress effectively, building resilience, fostering a positive mindset and seeking professional financial advice when needed, you can protect your mental well-being and make informed financial decisions.

In the next chapter, we will explore practical strategies for rebuilding and strengthening your financial foundation post-crisis, including rebuilding savings, repairing credit and setting new financial goals for the future.

# Chapter Eleven: Rebuilding Your Financial Foundation

Emerging from a financial crisis requires deliberate steps to rebuild and strengthen your financial foundation. This chapter delves into practical strategies for rebuilding savings, repairing credit and setting new financial goals for the future.

Start by assessing the impact of the financial crisis on your savings. Determine how much you have left and identify any emergency funds or savings that were depleted during the crisis.

Develop a new realistic budget that reflects your current income and expenses. Prioritize essential expenses such as housing, utilities, groceries and debt repayments. Allocate a portion of your income towards rebuilding your savings.

Establish short-term and long-term savings goals based on your financial priorities. Aim to build an emergency fund that covers at least three to six months' worth of living expenses. Break down larger goals into smaller, manageable milestones.

Automate transfers from your checking account to your savings or emergency fund. Setting up automatic contributions ensures consistency and removes the temptation to spend money earmarked for savings.

## Repairing Credit

Obtain a copy of your credit report from each of the major credit bureaus. Review your reports for inaccuracies, late payments or accounts in collections that may be impacting your credit score.

Dispute any inaccuracies or errors on your credit report. Contact creditors to negotiate repayment plans or settlements for outstanding debts. Making timely payments and reducing outstanding balances can improve your credit score over time.

Manage your credit responsibly to rebuild your credit history:

- **Pay bills on time.** Timely payments demonstrate financial responsibility and positively impact your credit score.

- **Reduce debt.** Focus on paying down existing debt to lower your credit utilization ratio, which can improve your credit score.

- **Limit new credit applications.** Avoid opening multiple new credit accounts, as each application can temporarily lower your credit score.

## Setting New Financial Goals

Use the financial crisis as an opportunity for reflection. Consider what worked well and areas where you can improve your financial habits and decisions.

Set new financial goals that align with your current priorities and aspirations. These may include saving for retirement, purchasing a home, starting a business or funding education expenses.

Create a detailed plan outlining the steps needed to achieve your goals. Break down each goal into actionable tasks, set deadlines and monitor your progress regularly.

Remain flexible in your financial planning. Economic conditions and personal circumstances may change, requiring adjustments to your goals and strategies.

Rebuilding your financial foundation after a crisis is a gradual process that requires discipline, patience and strategic planning. By focusing on rebuilding savings, repairing credit and setting new financial goals, you can regain financial stability and position yourself for future success.

# Conclusion: Navigating Financial Crises with Resilience

Congratulations on completing this journey through navigating financial crises with resilience and preparedness. Throughout this material, we have explored essential strategies and practical advice to help you manage and overcome financial challenges effectively.

From understanding the nature of financial crises to building a strong financial foundation, each chapter has equipped you with valuable insights and actionable steps. You have learned how to:

- **Prepare proactively.** By setting financial goals, diversifying income streams and managing debt effectively.

- **Adapt strategically**. By staying informed about economic trends, seeking professional advice and maintaining a positive mindset.

- **Rebuild Successfully.** By rebuilding savings, repairing credit and setting new financial goals post-crisis.

Financial resilience is more than just weathering storms — it's about thriving in the face of adversity. It's about leveraging your knowledge, skills and resources to bounce back stronger and more prepared for the future.

As you move forward, remember to:

- **Stay informed.** Continue educating yourself about financial matters and economic trends.

- **Be proactive.** Regularly review and adjust your financial plan as needed to align with your goals.

- **Seek support.** Whether from financial advisors, community resources or personal networks, don't hesitate to seek guidance when necessary.

Financial stability is a journey, not a destination. Embrace the lessons learned from past experiences and use them to shape a brighter financial future. By maintaining discipline, resilience and a forward-thinking mindset, you can navigate any financial challenges that lie ahead.

Thank you for investing in your financial well-being. May your path be filled with prosperity, resilience, and continued growth.

## About the Author

Ray Cyners specializes in weaving together the intricate worlds of Finance, Philosophy and Technology. With a keen eye for detail and a passion for uncovering the profound implications of economic trends, philosophical thought and technological advancements, Ray creates compelling narratives that both educate and inspire. His goal is to break down complex concepts into accessible, engaging content, making them a valuable resource for readers seeking to navigate the modern world's financial landscapes, ethical dilemmas and technological innovations.

www.ingramcontent.com/pod-product-compliance
Lightning Source LLC
Chambersburg PA
CBHW071958210526
45479CB00003B/986